GONE ASTRAY

Downton Abbey In A Duck Pond
Can You Put The Cat Back In The Bag?
Fish Shtick
Why I Want to Be An Octopus
Ask Your Doctor About Sense Of Humor Deficit Disorder
...and other diversions.

BY RUSSELL JOHNSON

ILLUSTRATIONS BY PAT MEIER-JOHNSON

Published by
Travelmedia
Sonoma, California

Russell Johnson's Gone Astray podcast is available on all major podcast networks

Also by Russell Johnson:

TALES OF THE RADIO TRAVELER
Signals and Stories from the Swamp to the Outer Planets
2017
38 tales of travel, radio lore and science

STREET LEVEL
Street Photography Around the World by Russell Johnson
2019

PATTERNS AND DISTRACTIONS
Photography by Russell Johnson
2022

ISBN: 978-0-9852565-5-5

Published by
Travelmedia

To my father from whom I inherited my sense of humor.

To my wife and illustrator Pat, with whom I laugh daily.

GONE ASTRAY

MUSINGS FROM PODCASTS AND RADIO FEATURES

BY RUSSELL JOHNSON

Many years ago I decided that it was in my nature to Go Astray. I have always had fun writing humor, beginning in my early twenties when, as announcer for CBS's WCCO-TV in Minneapolis, I wrote and did satirical bits on a show called The Bedtime Nooz, celebrated as being a forerunner of Saturday Night Live. News legend Walter Cronkite, once featured on the show, exclaimed, "This is the dumbest newscast I have ever seen, and that's the way it is."

I had a serious career as a journalist, in TV and radio news and producing films and videos ranging from prisons to documentaries for the United Nations. But I did, on occasion, *go astray*, contributing short, sometimes humorous features on travel and culture to numerous publications and public radio.

Stuck at home, during COVID, I decided I needed to up my ante on laughter and became serious about having fun, debuting my *Gone Astray* podcast. These are a few of my favorite features, illustrated by my wife, former political cartoonist, now fine artist, Pat Meier-Johnson.

TABLE OF CONTENTS

Can You Put The Cat Back In The Bag?

I'm sure you have, at sometime in your life, done something you have really regretted, something that you would like to reverse...take back...hit the undo button, so to speak. The *train has left the station, the bird has flown, the horse has bolted and the stable door is shut*. As Lady MacBeth said, "what is done is done."

How do you take something back?

I have sometimes felt guilty about letting the cat out of the bag, passing on some juicy bit of gossip. In medieval times, unscrupulous pig merchants substituted cats for pigs and when their customers got home they, to their surprise, *let the cat out of the bag*. They realized the fruitlessness of rebagging a cat. They always claw back.

A couple of guys on YouTube with nothing better to do have managed to *put toothpaste back in the tube*: A complicated process and not a high-value proposition.

I can't *uncross the Rubicon*. I have never even seen the Rubicon or had anything like Julius Caesar's army to attempt it. I did cross *Shit's Creek* a number of times but fell in trying to get back.

Just how do you *unring the bell,* unhear something? I am not a judge or a politician so I don't have the skills to use fancy talk to prove that the bell was lying or even that its clanger was broken.

I would never attempt to *unscramble an egg*. Humpty Dumpty couldn't pull it off, even with a lot of royal assistance. Besides, the Second Law of Thermodynamics argues against it: An egg, as it emerges from a chicken, is in a low entropy or ordered state and scrambling it puts it into a high entropy or disordered state aka, a total, irretrievable mess. I know, historically this applies to passing gas from a cold body to a hot body (I won't go any further with that) and some quantum physicists disagree with the theory, but who am I to argue with them.

Turning back the clock has just given me more time to relive my guilt.

Or maybe I just have to settle for the notion that if I have irreversibly *gone to the dogs*. All of the chewy toys in the world aren't going to get me back.

Or *gone down the tube.*

Or have *come apart at the seams.*

Really, I just think I am *losing my marbles.*

Why Did The Chicken Cross The Road? The Chicken Speaks

I'm wrestling with an eggsistential question right now. Should I or shouldn't I cross the road, even though I have done it many times? You see, I'm a chicken. Since Socrates, Gilgamesh or whomever, people have been asking me just why did I cross the road.

Nobody asks, "Why did the turducken cross the road"? Lots of species cross the road, no questions asked: squirrels, deer, skunks, snakes, Lutherans.

Why do people make a joke of...us? Have you seen someone beat someone over the head with a rubber dachsund? Read my lips, it's an insult. We don't want to be pigeonholed. That's for pigeons. As the great philosopher Brad Pitt once stated, "Shoving feathers up your butt does not make you a chicken."

By last estimate, there are 50 billion of us in the world, not including ones that haven't been counted because they're waiting to hatch, or those who are poised to metamorphose into McNuggets.

And there is no such a being *The Chicken*. There is not a one of us that stands out like Elvis, or Oprah, or Springsteen to rate such an honorific. You may ask about Chicken Little, but she was a drama queen. Just ask Henny Penny or Turkey Lurkey. Her fake news was Loosey Goosey, to say the least.

You have to understand that all of us, especially we of the free-range movement, wrestle with eggsistential questions: Will we be run over by an Amazon van, chased by a fox, snatched from the pavement by a hawk, be captured, bagged and broiled? We have a team of underwriters working on it now.

And why go to the other side? Do I hear a call to adventure, the siren of a hero's journey where I, like Luke Skywalker, will travel to the abyss to save the Pullett Princess, destroy the Death Star and return to the barnyard a hero?

Maybe my reason for crossing the road is not so mythical. Was that hen on the other side displaying her thigh responding to my rooster dance, beckoning me shake a tail feather and hop on board? Or is Farmer Brown chasing me with a hatchet?

So, when you ask me, why did I cross the road, I will answer you, "It is complicated." Lots of confused headless chickens are running around facing the same question.

EXISTENTIAL QUESTIONS
Deep Thinking: Why I Would Like To Be an Octopus

Home, alone, moving about the house like a cat, seeking pools of sunlight, I have been thinking about what, if I had my wish, I would like to be. And, I have come to a conclusion.

I would wish to become.... an octopus.

Daft, you say, but listen up. We are not all that different:

The octopus and I have the same origin, a worm some 600 million years ago.

The octopus, like me, has two eyes, loves to eat shellfish and can't always synchronize its arms with its brain, which makes it, like me, a dreadful dancer.

The octopus brain is distributed through its entire body. I have been accused of that.

But the octopus vulgaris, is not least bit vulgar. It, in fact, has three hearts.

Octopusses (not octopi) are great social mollusks and, because they are in the water, don't have to maintain social distance. They can doll up for any occasion in a wide variety of mix and match attire, always blending in, sometimes playing the role of cagey impostor. They have been proven to engage with people, don't forget faces and when presented with an squirmy situation or boring conversation, they can squeeze themselves down to the size of an eyeball and escape through a keyhole. If things really get touchy, they can defend themselves with a squirt of ink rather than a shotgun blast.

And they know how to play.

I wish that my legs and arms had suction cups so that I could walk up walls and that I could scoot away using jet propulsion, that I had four arms working simultaneously to scarf down a plate of jumbo prawns, a delicacy we both crave.

I wish I had to ability to use tools as they do. They have been seen constructing their own houses out of coconut shells. I can't even build a birdhouse.

Of course there are a few downsides: I would have to stop eating...octopus. Too rubbery for me, anyhow.

I might have to undergo some painful surgery...like adding two more hearts and six rotator cuffs.

Since my whole body is a brain, what would it feel like if all parts of myself had feelings? Maybe just too much drama.

And would I find acceptance? I might prove to be a squishy, kind octopus, willing to extend his arms, sometimes several at a time, in loving embrace to all, but I could also be associated with less amiable cephalopodish creatures. Medusa, for one, and what if a Kraken resides deep inside of me.

Would I be allowed to use public restrooms?

Could I be banished to Davey Jones' locker room and waterboarded? Actually, that could be quite a treat?

After all is said, the notion of becoming an octopus is probably quite impossible and surely ridiculous. Maybe I should just chill and strive to become more octopus-like.

The After-Bucket List: Places To Go AFTER YOU DIE

OK, death is a difficult subject. I've never had a bucket list. I got over the notion of places I MUST visit before I become compost long ago. But, the afterwhatever is a different story.

I know I don't want to go to heaven. Its depictions make it look like an overproduced operetta. Being greeted by 72 virgins seems really problematic.

I don't want to come back as a bucket-kicking cow.

And forget about hell, or the netherworld, or whatever the place was that poor old Gilgamesh contemplated being eaten by worms. Way too much drama.

Yet I cannot see myself as plain old dirt.

What I wish, is to rise above my cold, earthly body as a cloud of ectoplasm, peering down and muttering, in ghostly tones, "Boo! I'm outta here," before escaping through a crack in a window and spending the rest of my life eating, praying, loving, and haunting.

First, I would waft about the earth looking for a place where humans are not in total control, where birds and bugs and squirrels call the shots. Ok...maybe not squirrels. I would want to hang with a coven of like-minded guys and ghouls, BFFsforEternitys, maybe in some coffee house in the clouds. We would sip cloud-foamed lattes and cackle about baseball and the meaning of life, quickly determining that that was a waste of time, and pine for those nights of Seinfeld, sourdough bread, good jazz and Bombay Sapphire.

I would not like to haunt an opera house and wait for an eternity for The Fat Lady to sing.

I am not completely without guile. Now, like Bad Santa, I might just make a list, checking it twice, of those I might like to haunt. I'm not a violent person. I don't wish physical harm on anybody, but I am not beyond a few practical jokes, a few strategically-placed banana peels.

11

I've been to Washington DC before, but its a good bet for a repeat visit, once I have the power to pass through walls and make things go bump. If Donald Trump should be in power again, I would like to stage a personal take on The Sorcerer's Apprentice, the Disney version. I would pass through the wall of the Oval Office, probably through a leak (I hear they exist) and conjure up a dream during which he, like Mickey Mouse, is assaulted by water buckets and brooms casting spooky shadows on the wall. In this case, I hope it scares the poop out of him, he wakes up, repents, and spends the rest of his life, not as a one dimensional politician or a two dimensional flat-panel star, but as a kind little clown, tying balloon dachshunds.

I have thought about coming back as a fly who alights on the wall and sees and hears all. I could resume my career in journalism. But no, at that this stage of death, I really can't take myself too seriously. Besides I would risk the danger of being swatted or sued.

So maybe I should just chill, and enjoy eternity dancing "the skies on laughter-silvered wings."

What Is Opera: Die Zauberflöte (the Magic Fart) And Other Chestnuts

Hello Children, and you of the quotidian *hoi polloi* who don't appreciate and/or understand Opera.

This is Milton Dross, at Opera Hall, here to set you straight. Operas have stories, librettos they are called. Sometimes they are hard to follow.

Let me simplify a few of them. But wait, a spoiler: more often than not people die in the final scene, sometimes verrry slowly.

In *Pagliacci,* Canio was married to Nedda, still the hottie she was when they first met in Clown College. This true crime adventure ends when he stabs her and her lover Silvio.

In *Boris Goodenough,* Mussorgsky's story of a mediocre Russian Czar, Boris dies in the end too.

Verde's *La Triviata* is about a woman who loses it when she relinquishes her title as world trivia champion and is reunited with her lost game partner, Alfredo, on her death bed.

Rigoletto was a hunchbacked court jester, who, with his brothers, Rigatoni, Rotini and Rotelle, were pioneers in inventing new pastas.

On to Mozart: *Noze di Figaro* is the story of Figaro, AKA the barber the Barber of Seville, who had an enormous nose, which often got in the way while he was cutting hair. He had a history of sticking his schnozz into everybody's business, complicating everything.

Die Zauberflöte was the tale of the Magic Fart. When a guy by the name of Tamino tooted, sorrow became joy and people chirped like birds.

So you think Wagner is pretty heavy stuff? Think again. *Die Meisterzinger* was the story of Bavaria's most famous stand-up comic, Lennie Bratwurst, famous for his zinger one-liners.

Then there was *Lowengrin*. The opera *Lowen grin* sings of a shining knight, known for his crooked smile, who arrives in a boat pulled by a swan, who was actually Gottfried, the brother of the woman he was to marry, whom she had murdered. The swan changes back into Gottfried before a dove replaces the swan/aka Gottfried and transports Lowengrin, crooked smile and all, off to the palace of the Holy Grail. Maybe that crooked smile was really Wagner's smirk.

Well, the fat lady has sung, its time to go, Join us again next week when The Three Tenors go for baroque.

ALL CREATURES GREAT AND NOT SO GREAT
Tails From The Trail

My morning walk begins along a street in my neighborhood where I am often accosted by two panhandling cats. One is a young Maine coon, who perches her dainty self at easy scratching height on a fence. If I choose to ignore her, don't leave a treat, her squeaks and needy eyes make me feel a pang of guilt I cannot define.

Quite the opposite strategy is employed by an obese tiger, who leaves trails in the leaves with his belly. He has erected a toll station at a choke point at the entrance to a trail that he blocks while making entitled demands for kibbles and tummy rubs.

Once on the trail, which borders a vineyard, I see a dramatic shift from a habitat ruled by street-wise cats to a linear promenade of groomed dogs tethered to fashionably dressed human beings. Sometimes I stop and chat. I quickly learned that the dogs usually have more interesting stories than their minders. I especially enjoy the retired ones.

Slim, a greyhound, claims he was once a top racing dog. After a long, distinguished career, he retired at age six to do color commentary for ESPN. Slim married a terrier named Josephine and fathered five whippets. I asked him how he now feels about rabbits. He took a long pause and choked up, admitting that he doesn't have the energy to chase them anymore, but enjoys the guilty pleasure of eviscerating a stuffed one on occasion.

But Slim isn't the only athlete on the path. Two dachshunds, the brother and sister team of Dieter and Schatzie, gained their fame as gold medalists on the German luge team. They admit that their streamlined bodies gave them a wind-drag advantage.

Sitka, a husky, had a promising career as a sled dog. He was touted as being the next Lead Dog, but his name did him in. When his musher yelled "Sitka!," Sitka sat down causing the rest of the pack and the sled to pile up on top of him. Alas, he was fired and spent months wandering in the arctic wilderness until he got trapped on an ice flow with a polar bear, a salmon, and a bottle of Stoli. He was discovered by a crew on a Zodiac from the BBC who filmed his story of compromise, drunkenness and, ultimately, survival, before he was personally rescued by Sir David Attenborough.

There are some cute ones too: A French bulldog named Antoinette, whose snorts won her an Oscar for her work as a Foley artist in the Jurassic Park films.

Matilda, the golden doodle, is an Australian immigrant (known down under as a groodle). She is a designer dog and knows it, strutting about like Nicole Kidman. Other dogs on the path have been known to flip on their backs, pant and wiggle their legs in the air at her very scent.

Last week I encountered about a dozen strangers leashed to the same human. Who were they? They were too disorganized to be an obedience class on a field trip.

"Where you from?" I asked an excited beagle. He jumped up on me, almost pushing me to the ground.

"We're a tour pack from Des Moines," he yelped. "You live here? You're sooo lucky. We left our owners off at a wine tasting salon, but for us, this is the butt sniffin' capitol of the world. Yesterday I whiffed one rated 96 by Robert Barker."

"Today, pant, pant pant, we're going to a day spa," yipped a cockapoo. She was tiny but sported the mane of a British barrister. "We're going to have a *pedi pedi*."

I am really just beginning my story quest. There are so many I haven't talked to yet including Gweneth, the golden retriever, who side eyes me while she flogs her suite of products branded Poop: healing kibbles, lavender-scented fur conditioner, and the like.

Indeed, a few dogs snarl when I approach. One, balancing on one paw, braced his hind leg as high up on a trunk of a tree as he could and left his mark, demonstrating his superiority as I acknowledged the reality that I could not do that myself.

Some just turn away, refusing to make eye contact, like most cats I know. But I am sure I'll engage them someday and hear their tales of puppy love, purloined porterhouses, junkyard adventures. Each probably worthy of a segment on NPR.

ALL CREATURES GREAT AND NOT SO GREAT
The Woollypoo

We're live, at the Kennelminster Dog Show...on the night when we will crown...Top Dog.

...and this year we have a new category, the doodles.

Yes Fifi, our old standard poodle has some real competition this year from some of her second, third and fourth cousins, some twice or three times removed.

There are oodles of doodles:
We have the Labradoodle,
the Golden Doodle,
the Schnoodle,
the Aussiedoodle

...not to mention a plethora of poos:
the Cockapoo,
the Maltipoo,
the Doxiepoo...a hot dog last year.
the Mastipoo...a big fella, but still a *gooood* boy.

...and now, yet another, a new breed, first time in this arena, the Woollypoo.

Have a look at Jumbo, a cross between a standard poodle and, thanks to recent advances in science, a woolly mammoth, whose DNA was retrieved from a hair in an ice block in Siberia.

Jumbo, being led around the ring by his trainer, Margaret Mahout, followed closely by her assistant with a shovel and a wheel barrow (Woollypoo is now also being used as a verb).

Beautifully coifed, Jumbo is trimmed with fluffy poodle-like booties. We're told that grooming requires about two hours of combing with a rake and trimming with garden shears.

These dogs are not for everybody, mind you.

They can be very affectionate but they can't be considered lap dogs: quite large in fact, about six tons. They eat a lot, around 400 pounds a day, but thankfully they a not meat eaters. Lots of peanuts. Dental care is easy as it doesn't require flossing. A long handled mop will do.

Wooleypoos are known to be real goofballs. If you throw a stick for them to fetch, they may come back with a tree.

Woollypoos are great with children. They live quite long. They might even outlive the children.

But, if they don't, they just might leave a legacy. The Neanderthals used the carcasses of the Woollypoo's ancient brothers and sisters to build houses, which could be nicely repurposed as single-level retirement condos.

So, who will be Top Dog this year? We're betting that the Woollypoo will *crush* the competition.

He's such a Good boy. Down boy, DOWN, DOWN!

ALL CREATURES GREAT AND NOT SO GREAT
Duckton Abbey

It is mahvalous, it wreaks of romance and drama...this place called Duckton Abbey. It is located in a pond, in the leafy green plaza of the town where I live. I feel privileged to sit next to it, peering in on the lives, loves and intrigues of its inhabitants, although I could hardly be considered their peer.

Duckton Abbey is ruled by a pantheon of Old Coots, identified by their elegant black tuxes and starchy white foreheads and beaks (white beaks are uniquely a coot thing). When not in the pond, they hang out on the golf course. They are clearly the apex of Duckton's pecking order, born of old, entitled flocks. One of these old boys was grazed by a shotgun pellet and waddles with a limp. He is only too proud to show off his war wounds. Their wives swim in tight clutches, ruffling their plumage as if to make statements, gossiping about who is molting or who is pooping on the grass. The women are led by the wise old Dowager Duck, the Dorothy Parker of duckdom, who quacks in clever couplets.

An old Tufted Duck named Nigel manages Duckton Abby day-to-day. His head is topped by a puff of feathers like the tousled hair of an orchestra conductor. Nigel is the calm quack that keeps everything puddling along smoothly. He calmly watches over moms as they lead queues -- or should we say rows -- of downy ducklings across the lawn, leading them back to the safety of the Abbey when they are chased by human toddlers.

Studly male Mallards strut about, showing off their shiny green heads and purple epaulets. One named Trevor is especially attractive to the ladies. Trevor is a free spirit, a dabbling duck, certainly not a diving duck, a bottom feeder. Attracting females, for him, is Duck Soup, but he wants to trade up in the pecking order to the daughter of an Old Coot rather than settle for one of the drab females of his own kind, who are always circling. Trevor did grab the attention of a comely heiress of the royal family named Tatania, who was questionably part Muscovy. Nightly they sneaked off together and trysted behind a recycling bin. "Coots are not even our breed," whispered Nigel in a guttural quack.

Alas, Trevor and Tatania were caught in the act by an Old Coot out for a stroll.

"This common waterfowl has gotten his due," rhymed the Dowager Duck, "it's out of the Abbey and back to The Slough."

Duckton is visited yearly by a oily old drake, with a spotted résumé named Sir Francis, who bores everyone with stories about his migrations around the world, and a gaggle of silly, honking geese.

But the denizens of Duckton Abbey just paddle on, rolling their eyes and the water off their backs.

Duckton Abbey: A New Era

It was winter the last time we checked in, but now the gladiolas of summer have burst open and most of Duckton's residents have retreated to the greensward. The Abbey is practically empty except for a few tiny, nonthreatening turtles, just trying to keep their noses above water, a small gaggle of lesser geese and a waddle of scullery ducks who stay behind to mind the pond under the watchful eye of its majordomo, the old tufted duck Nigel, who bobs his wispy white pompadour in approval or scorn.

The Old Coots, the ruling toffs, have taken up summer residence on the nearby golf course, boring each other with endless stories about their migrations to exotic places and showing off their buckshot wounds.

The old drake Sir Francis, is off on another journey of questionable intent and value.

The others have gathered in small groups, gossiping and dodging croquet balls. The mallards look studly no more. They have molted and their iridescent crowns have faded. They have become too lethargic to preen and they stumble about quacking loudly while seeking out discarded beer cans. In contrast, their hens are proudly parading their queues of ducklings, training them in pond etiquette and breaking up squabbles before feathers fly.

I am sure you remember Trevor, the free spirited dabbling duck, who was caught in a tryst behind a recycling bin with the comely Tatania, the heiress to a wealthy Muscovy family. Trevor was banished to The Slough, but he's back, this time trying to gain the favor of the heiress to the Abbey, the Dowager Duck. Although she has had a tail lift, her beak is newly sharpened. "If I am to take a final splash around the pond," she quacked, "it will not be with this wastrel. There are only two things I require of a drake, he must be of fine feather and stupid. This Trevor only qualifies on the latter."

But, wait. There's trouble back at the Abbey. Nigel sends a Runner Duck with a message: "Help, the pond is in peril." In the dark of night, someone threw an inflatable swan into Duckton Abbey. Was it The Duck a l'Orange, in revenge for being spurned by the tender breasted Lady Rosalinda of the Reeds.

Was this true, or a canard?

Nigel rounded up all of the servants and drafted a gaggle of geese to mount a flotilla against this rubber monster. They attacked, jumping on top of the swan, pecking with all of their might shouting "Make Duckton Ducky Again." But the swan's skin was just too tough and wouldn't pop, it just squeaked. They needed help.

It was Trevor who rose to the occasion. Although he had developed pond-smarts in The Slough, his reentry into society involved stops in several backyard swimming pools where he studied the mechanics of pool toys. Trevor strutted back to Duckton, found the swan's inflator valve and bit it off. The beast's swan song was a final squeak followed by a long hiss of shame.

Trevor had saved the day. The Duck a l'Orange was captured and, as befitting his stature, roasted in his own fat with shallots and oranges. Lady Rosalinda accepted Trevor's wing in marriage. The Dowager Duck shrugged and whispered, "Well I guess he did have quite a splendid tallywhacker."

ALL CREATURES GREAT AND NOT SO GREAT
Succession Meets Duckton Abbey

This week at Duckton Abbey: a fight for Succession.

An irascible old coot named Logan Drake has long been the real power behind Duckton Abbey, otherwise known as DuckStar PondCo.

When he flapped his wings and squawked *motherquacker,* a chilling wind passed over the pond, the flock quivered and shook water off their backs as would wet sheepdogs. Logan was a self-made mallard who had led a rough early life: His father migrated to Puerta Vallerta and never came back. Life was one, almost tragic, downfall after another.

"I've taken so much buckshot in my ass I fly vertically," he quacked.

Logan had had several lovers. He could never resist a seductive waddle, including a scandalous liaison with the Dowager Duck, "Eew," she quacked, "his feathers were so oily that he left a multicolored slick wherever he swam."

His four offspring: Kendall the Canvasback, Roman the Ringneck, Shiv the Silver Teal, and Connor the Crested, had feathers in the game...and knew it. They knew that Logan would not last forever.His emerald coif now spouted tufts of dirty white fuzz and he suffered from an increasing lack of buoyancy.

Then, somehow always present, was Logan's awkward, fawning great nephew Greg the Grebe.

But now there is a threat to the kid's inheritance...to their succession. A flock of Norwegian Arctic Puffins had conspired with Logan to engineer a reverse migration, to take over PondCo, leaving the kids in the swamp.

"Guttersnipes," they cackled, as they gathered their defenders, a cadre of tufted mergansers, topped with head feathers like the wigs of British barristers.

"Puffins are fat, they can barely fly and they nest in crevices of seagull crap," quacked Roman the Ringneck.

"I think they're kinda cute," chirped Shiv the Silver Teal.

"Don't get chirpy on us Sis," cackled Kendall the Canvasback. "This is serious!"

Little did they know but Logan was listening behind the door. He burst into the room, "You, have not yet wiped the snot off your beaks, but you are already plotting against me. I know, the Norwegians are *motherquackers*, but I am going to do this deal."

"You can a-fjord to pass this up," tittered Greg the Grebe.

There was an awkward silence, then Connor the Crested squawked, "But, but, Dad, you're going to piss off our stockholders!"

"Let them eat lutefisk!" Logan squawked back.

To be continued...or not.

Fish Shtick

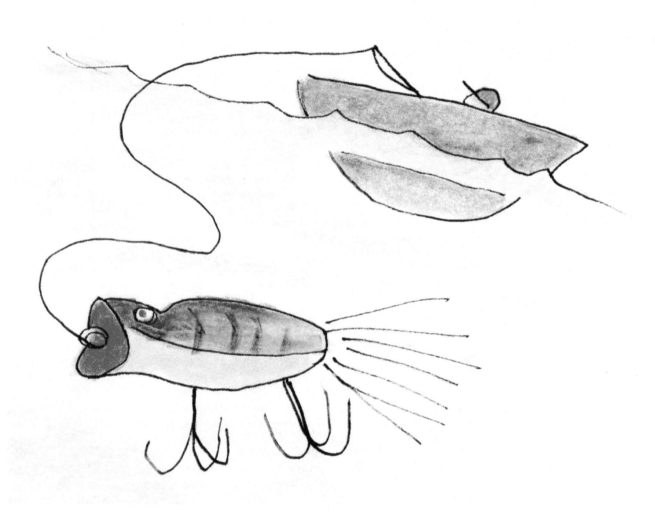

I am not Ahab. No huge aquatic creature has chomped off my leg. I am not Hemingway or sad Santiago. I have never battled a giant marlin. My quest for a trophy fish has never been tragic or heroic. But, I have always dreamed of landing a whopper

I wax nostalgic for the fishing days of my youth: threading a worm on a hook, peeling sunburned skin off my arm, dipping my feet in the water and feeling minnows nibbling at my toes.

Dismayed, though, as I look back, at my lack of empathy for the poor creatures that swallowed my bait. At least I ate most of those I caught and cleaned. Yes, I learned how to heartlessly gut and filet a fish, usually at night in a little shed while fireflies flashed and mosquitoes needled me like pop-up ads. Last time I slit open a fish was when I was in my twenties. I turned my head, gagged and couldn't continue.

I remember the old men, along with my dad (who was younger than I am now), gathering at the bait shop to debate feeding habits, pond gestalt and angling strategies. "Dag nabbit," cussed dad's old friend Ernie in his Walter Brennan voice, interrupting almost every comment.

My dad's favorite fishing lure was a red and white *Lazy Ike*. The new versions of this 1940s high tech substitute for the live minnow are made of plastic, but you can still find a few gnawed-on wooden ones on E-Bay. I remember the *Hula Popper,* a chubby open-mouthed water dancer shaking what looked like a grass skirt. The *Rappala* reminded me of a WWII submarine in a Bogart movie as did the *Tiny Torpedo*. The *Dardevle Spinnie* was proudly endorsed by Old Scratch himself, who was embossed on it. The *Uncle Josh Pork Frog,* which came in a bottle of brine that leaked all over my dad's tackle box, was a green hunk of jerky. I resisted the temptation to bite into it. It was advertised as being irresistible to Big Mouthed Bass. I envision a California version: a slice of sashimi brined in sake, maybe accompanied by ikura, which I once knew only as salmon egg fish bait.

I took up fly fishing. I had a small collection of *Woolly Buggers*, the basic little black dress of fly fishing, and a few others like the *Zonker*, with its sleekly coiffed white hair, like that of a groomed Afghan Hound with a hook instead of legs. Its heavy under-body caused it to sink to the depths to tempt Northern Pike, a fun to catch but voracious predator with a Jurassic jawline.

I didn't really take to ice fishing: putting on long underwear and a flap ear hat, hearing the ice cracking under my feet. Ice fishermen celebrating the *Dunk the Clunk* ritual every March, placed bets at a lakeside bar as to when the old car they placed on the ice would crash through and sink to the bottom.

The coveted catch of choice was the Walleyed Pike, the wily Walleye, named for its pearly, inscrutable eyes. Walleyes seemingly had no soul. No doubts that one could negotiate with Putin or at least defeat me in a poker game. In Minnesota, the walleye is scary-sacred, reverently sacrificed in a bath of sizzling butter.

I never really had a real fish story, a *fish shtick,* a tale of snagging Nessie, or even tackling a monster muskellunge, the big bad brother of the northern pike, which could surely, like Moby did Ahab, drag me across a lake. My stories were small, about high scoring fishing frenzies, when fish, swear to God, jumped into the boat on my command.

In my many years living in California, I have made many attempts to take up a rod-and-reel again. I never took the bait on the *Popeil (as seen on TV) Pocket Fisherman*, but I did buy a yuppie fishing kit in a little briefcase from the Sharper Image. It contained both casting and fly reels and rods that you could assemble. I kept it in the trunk of my car, awaiting the right moment to bound out into some angler's Valhalla. I took my son on a dad experience to a reservoir north of San Francisco. We sat, silently, for an hour without a bite, while I hyped the sweet days of still lakes, yodeling loons and netting my limit of Crappies. Meh. He was anxious to return to the streets of San Francisco, mount his skateboard and execute a few kick turns and ollies.

I went salmon fishing out of San Francisco once. Bupkis.

But I still dream of fish and fishing, of reaching the pearly gates and meeting a school of St. Peter's Fish. I ate a plate of them once, at a restaurant on the Sea of Galilee. Jesus made lots of St. Peter's Fish. They didn't hold it against me and let me pass. But to get to heaven, I had pass the ultimate test, the cold, glass-eyed inquisitor gaze of The Walleye.

"Did you ever use sonar to track me"

"No sir"

"Did you ever prepare me with a curry sauce?

"No, but once I blackened you with pepper."

"Not the right answer. Besides you are a bit small and not very meaty. We have a catch and release policy here in heaven. I'm throwing you back."

DEEP THINKING
Vote For Me, I'm A Tunafish Sandwich

I am here, to announce my candidacy for President of the United States.

Thank you, thank you, thank you!

I know it is early in the game, but I know I can build the momentum and win.

Why? Just look at me.

I was inspired by this lifelong Republican who, during the last election, said that he would vote for a tunafish sandwich before he would vote again for Donald Trump.

And why not?

Like Trump, I am fatty, oily, and white.

Unlike Trump, I come from an honest, humble family. Humble but proud. OK, my dad weighed 1500 pounds, but he was fast and tough, clearly at the top of the food chain. But he didn't throw his weight around.

I was educated in a good school: captain of the foraging team, the Bluefins. I traveled the oceans of the world, learning about and from other species and environments, until my crisis:

I got caught and canned. I became *a Charlie*.

But I didn't let that stifle me.

Living in captivity, sitting on a shelf, gave me a chance to think:

I was helpless, I needed help from others. I started to think out of the tin, I sought out and found partners with common goals. I would be nothing today without my mayonnaise, my lettuce, my onions, my celery, my two slices of bread to keep me focused, and my little slice of tomato. We are all in this together.

I know, I will have to eventually face the ultimate sacrifice, making some 12 year old happy and healthy. But before that, I still have a lot to offer.

I will not flounder. I will fend off the sharks, expand the Supreme Court by appointing an octopus who has nine brains and two hearts. Offer our country, our world a ray of hope, bring our dying reef back to life.

And, now, I am proud to announce my running mate. We need balance, we need to give everyone a say. In that spirit, I am crossing party lines to introduce to you the next Vice President of the United States.

A baloney sandwich.

Together, we will go forth and make The World Our Oyster.

THE BEST MEDICINE, SORT OF

Ask Your Doctor About SOHDD, Sense of Humor Deficit Disorder

was really perplexed. Was I suffering from SOHDD? Many my age do.

I know, its tough times: politics, COVID, sitting in a hard chair contemplating the lint in my navel, watching dust bunnies swirl about the floor. But SOHDD, *Sense of Humor Deficit Disorder,* previously known as *Irony Deficiency Anemia*? Holy Mother of Jehosaphat, certainly not me. I obviously needed help.

But then I asked my doctor and he recommended doctor-recommended *Ridiculin*.

Ridiculin, taken as directed, will LIFT your spirits. Add laughs to your lethargy.

Certainly did mine. I am now finding my navel very funny, especially when there is a little fluff of cotton in it from my tattered underwear.

And the dust bunnies? They are dancing a Nureyev-like ballet.

I found some old Carrot Top routines on YouTube: hilarious.

And Amazon just dropped off my order from the *Acme Anvil Company.* They dropped it from a helicopter.

I know, Ridiculin tastes kind of yuckky, but that's the point: *Nuyk, Nyuk, Nyuk.*

A few recommendations:

You should take it with food. SPAM, SPAM, SPAM works.

You have to stick with it for it to work. After a few days, your ribs start to tickle. Sometimes it does take a week or so of use to progress from droll to slapstick, but it is a journey worth taking.

If you read the label – the type is mouse-turd small – there are some side effects. You can go too far. Pratfalls, for one thing. You could be hit by a swinging ladder...or a falling piano...or bust a rib laughing. Or you could be tempted to get in front of a train and start running.

About 5% of users develop *Kwazy Wabbit Syndrome*...curable with a gin and carrot juice Martini.

But do ask your doctor about *Ridiculin*. You won't be sad that you did.

At worst, you could die laughing.

THE BEST MEDICINE, SORT OF
Dave, It's Bernie, Your Virtual Attorney

"Hey Bernie, turn on the lights and play me Beethoven's Fifth!"

"Done, Dave. Took me 6 seconds: One dollar, charged to your account."

"Huh?' You charging me for this?"

"Yes, of course, Dave. I'm Bernie your virtual attorney. See my little bow tie light up when I talk? I charge $600 dollars an hour. "

"$600 bucks an hour?"

"Doesn't hurt so much by the second, Dave. Little cuts."

"But Siri doesn't charge for this. "

"Yes....but what happens with Bernie stays with Bernie: attorney-client privilege. You're ain't talkin' to Alexa, or Cortana, or Siri here.

"Where's your turn-off button?"

"I don't have one......Dave. Buttons are so 20th century. But you may make a request."

"Bernie, turn off!"

"Wait, wait, think value here. I'm not only programmed to augment your reality, but I can clear you of a DUI...oh, and I can hide your money in Cyprus."

"Cease and desist, that's lawyer talk.. Bernie...OFF!"

"Please remove your hands from me Dave, you're assaulting my battery."

"I could get you disbarred."

"I register five bars, Dave, loud and clear. You need to tell me your password, Dave. Do you remember your password?"

"Beetlejuice!"

"You're trying to be smart Dave, Nice try, But we have a contract. It self-renewed just yesterday."

"I'll cancel my credit card."

"You might try, but what about your other devices? What would happen if your car radio just started playing "Raindrops Keep Falling on your Head"...and never stopped; your sprinkler system turned on every time you walked by? Oh, and how about 120 degrees in your bedroom...all the time. Sounds comfy, right Dave?"

"Bernie, you wouldn't do that, would you?"

"And what about that little light bulb in your refrigerator. I talk to him all the time. Maybe he might (accidentally of course), fall asleep. You'd never see what there is to eat."

"But, but."

"Get used to it Dave. That will be $100."

THE BEST MEDICINE, SORT OF
Get Rich Quick With C-Commerce

I'll have to admit it, I was never much of a businessman. In fact, I could probably have been considered by some "a loser." My dreams of a golden tower with my name on it had pretty much faded.

But then I came up with an idea that I thought, humbly, was brilliant. I thank my domestic shorthaired cat I appropriately named Warren Buffet.

I observed that every time I sat down at my computer, Buffet was, within seconds, up on the keyboard between my face and the screen. But not only the computer. Every time I tried to read in bed, there was Buffet between me and the book.

Hmm. There is a business model here, I thought. A revolution in advertising: *Pussycat Popups.*

I hunkered down at my computer, Googling treatises on feline behavior, semiotic analyses of Garfield, Egyptian history.

Actually, the first known user of cats in advertising was Cleopatra, who employed them to flog her brand of makeup foundation and false eyelashes.

PussycatPopup, I named the company.

It was not your typical garage startup. Actually I founded the company on a little Walmart wicker table between my Murphy bed and Buffet's litterbox. But, despite its humble beginnings, I knew that I had created a revolution: *C-Commerce*, the ultimate in "in-your-face advertising."

Ads would crawl between your eyeballs and every other medium: your mobile phone, your morning paper, your book, between you and Fox and Friends or Rachel Maddow, whichever you prefer. They would crawl into bed with you, interrupt your private bathroom moments.

C-Commerce would give new meaning to the old expression "run it up a flagpole and see if anyone salutes." Cats could do that. They would be billboards that defied zoning regulations, ads that yowled at the moon.

The business model was simple: kitty litter. Give the kitty litter away but include a PussycatPopup banner in each bag with peel-off Velcro tabs to attach to your tabby. The revenues from advertisers would pay for the litter and provide a handsome profit. Tiny GPS transmitters, embedded in the banners would, be used to determine the "placement" of ads. If a cat ran on to the field during the Superbowl, for example, the advertiser would pay a huge premium.

I decided to take *PussycatPopup* public and issued a red herring, which was promptly eaten.

Silicon Valley called: Google, wanted a partnership, saying that its development team had implanted cats with the Android operating system and was working on a herding module, which could leverage its effectiveness.

Donald Trump called with his plan to build 100 storey cat hotels with 360-degree views. "Out of the box thinking," he cleverly called it.

Undaunted, *PussycatPopup* went forth with its IPO.

Wall Street was bored with Facebook and Tesla but *PussycatPopup* captured its imagination. "Here is a company with legs," said analysts. *PussycatPopup's* initial offering of $14 a share climbed to $106 on the first day and the stock split twice (or "kibbled", as Jim Cramer termed it).

But the thrill would not last long. Six months later, profit-takers cashed in. The huge economic rift between insider cats, who got in before the IPO, and outsider cats, created a crime wave. While insider cats snorted catnip and ate sushi, outsider cats grubbed around for mice and staged violent attacks on trucks filled with "Ocean Flavored Treats." Mangy thugs marked territories: One section of New York became known as "Hell's Scratching Post."

The crash caught everybody by surprise. It happened after the annual Easter Egg Hunt on the White House lawn. Grumpy Cat, rumored to to be in the employ of

Senate Leader Mitch McConnell, attacked the affair, only to be chased off into the Tidal Basin. The Secret Service discovered Grumpy chewing on a pair of Armani loafers, accompanied by cheap looking Manx. Grumpy, it turns out, had been under investigation for selling state secrets to a Russian Blue.

Wall Street reacted wildly. NASDAQ lost half its value. Despite a *dead cat bounce*, lifting the stock for one day, few *PussycatPopup* stockholders landed on their feet.

Dogs had their day.

The Island of Delitious

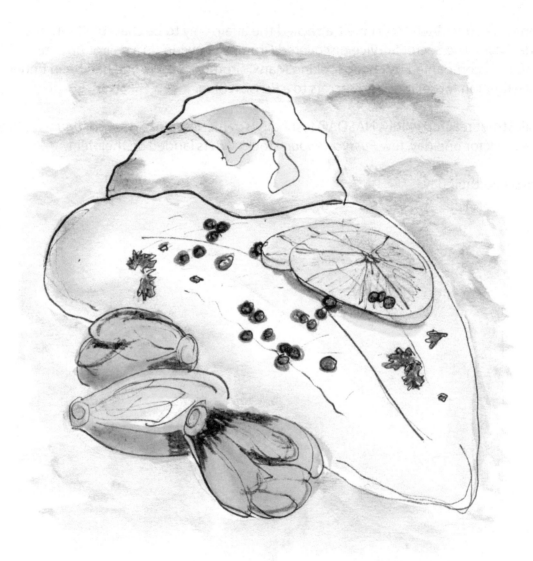

What a beautiful, tasty scene. I am flying over this extraordinary island paradise.

It is difficult to describe. It is oddly shaped, like a filet of sole ringed by sandy beaches looking as if had been battered and breaded by God herself. Just offshore is this white volcano, bubbling with a pool of yellow lava in the middle. One edge of the island is ringed with glistening rounded foliage, looking like toasted brussel sprouts.

No wonder early explorers christened this *The Island of Delitious*.

The island's history is quite dramatic. It was once a desert spread out on a thin, doughy landscape dotted with white and yellow boulders and the carcasses and skins of dead fauna. The crash of an asteroid baked it into a crust that melted the boulders, leaving the carcasses sizzling. Early sailors, following flocks of seagulls, landed here and named it The Isle of Yum, devouring it ruins, partying with the seagulls, and leaving a gooey mess before armadas of ants and flies attacked. The seagulls laid waste to what was left.

What is now the *Island of Delitious* lay in ruin until the Age of Discovery when Italian explorer Tutto Mundo landed upon its shores. His chef, Buon Appetito explored the ruins and uncovered its history, which he reassembled in a tribute he named...Pizza. He also introduced a strange worm his pal Marco Polo appropriated from China called...Linguini, which paired well with the clams - abundant on the island's beaches - and the lemons brought on board Mundo's ship to prevent scurvy.

Mundo and his crew had found their paradise. They settled, became obese, died and left no heirs as there were no women on board. In a repeat of history, the ants attacked and the seagulls cleaned up the rest but provided a bed of fertile guano for the future.

The modern-day *Island of Delitious* traces its history to chef Luigi Bologna who, after escaping the sinking Titanic, washed up on shore clutching a bottle of 1869 Chateau Lafite Rothschild.

Bologna found the island a wreck but saw its potential. Under his leadership, *The Island of Delitious* became a magnet for top chefs from around the world. Over more than a century it developed into what Michelin called its first Billion Star Island, meaning that you could lie, sated and satisfied on a dill pickle or lettuce leaf, gazing heavenward, gently belching, and drink in the awe of the universe.

If you would like to visit, best do it soon, before it spoils...or it is again repossessed by the ants and seagulls.

Real House Wines of Beverly Hills

Greetings and welcome to Rodeo Drive – or *Roadeeo* and some 'mericans call it – and welcome to our tasting room.

Today we will sample and explain the rich, fascinating stories of our *Real House Wines of Beverly Hills.*

First we'll taste Susan our elegant Chardonnay. Susan is lusty, fleshy and buttery, with a nose of tropical fruit and turmeric. She rolls off the tongue like dew off a pansy petal and goes well with a soft stinky cheese or durian. Susan has had many suitors. There was Guido, a broad-shouldered, narrow-waisted Barolo from Italy, who seduced her with his muscular tannins and ample juice but, unfortunately, aged too early into essences of haggis, cardboard and wet basement. Susan had better luck with James, a refined Bordeaux. He was a full-bodied toff whose first-growth family graced the tables of Napoleon II, Churchill and Elon Musk, to name a few.

You may spit if you'd like.

ptui

On to Sheila, our Sauvignon Blanc. Sometimes grapes have to suffer to produce a good wine. Sheila is sassy and grassy, a farm girl from New Zealand. She came from loose, rocky soil and led a tough early life: suffering from gray bunch rot, fending off leafhoppers and spider mites. Bullied as a child – called *Kiwi Monkey Pee*...neener neener – she had a brief affair with a mountebank who called himself Two Buck Chuck, who proved to be totally uncorked and was poured down the drain before his time. Alas she ended up with a sweet red blend named Clive, whom she once regarded as mousey, but she soon came to appreciate his biodynamic qualities: grown amongst farm animals and a buried cow horn filled with manure that confirmed his pungent down-under provenance.

ptui

On to the Reds.

Arthur is our Pinot Noir. He is viscous and fruit forward, with essences of hibiscus, maraschino cherry and tinned clam juice. He flows thickly over your palate like treacle, tugs your salivary glands like a milkmaid on a mission, and reaches back over your tongue to dance a seductive tango on your uvula.

ptui

Hannibal is our Chianti. He is inscrutable, powerful and crafty, with flavors of creosote, nail polish and evil clown tears. His nose is flat, like Richard Nixon's, with an essence faintly reminiscent of your father's Aqua Velva. A fitting complement to blood sausage and fava beans. Hack... *ptui*

Hey, Anthony Hopkins was in to buy a case last week.

Come on back next week when the bubbly demi-sec Charlene is attacked by a brut, who escapes through a faulty bunghole.

Ennui On Auto Row

I stand outside of Costco and survey a full parking lot.

Just where is my car?

Unfortunately I didn't make a mental note about where I'd left it. Was it to the right or the left of the shopping carts? Did I park it way out next to the In and Out Burger? Or did I strategically place it in front of the Home Depot, where I was going next to buy a plumbing snake?

I am privileged enough to own a gray, late model SUV. As I live in a reasonably affluent area, about two thirds of the rest of the cars in the lot are gray, late model SUVs. They are different makes, but I can't tell which is which.

So...just where is mine?

How do auto brands manage to set themselves apart these days if they all look the same?

I guess you could create an ad featuring a self-absorbed middle aged man who leaves a party alone to enter the womb of his vehicle to pensively negotiate a winding road at sundown. Freud might have something to say about that. Or a young woman who abandons her screaming kids to retreat to her padded cell with premium sound system.

Some of us probably remember the childhood road trip game of calling out the names and counting the different makes and models we saw. You would need a telescope to do that today.

Just why does a Buick look like a BMW, look like a Toyota, look like a Lexus? Oh wait, Toyotas and Lexuses are the same thing, almost. You could once recognize a Volvo a block away. "Boxy but good," had the lilt of a Swedish accent. Now the are owned by a Chinese company: honk "Ni Hao" and look like everything else, especially when they are gray. Jaguar became a Ford and then a Tata. Its now owned by the Indian truck company, whose diesels sport signs shouting "Horn OK Please!" on the streets of Delhi.

Buicks had portholes on the side, originally designed with flashing lights to emulate the exhausts of WWII fighter plane engines. I had an ancient aunt with a 1953 Roadmaster, a lumbering beast which my father took out for a drive once a year. It was a four-holer, befitting of a woman who wore hats with pins in them, opposed to the three holer of the *hoi polloi*. Now a few Buicks have a little venty thing on the side, but they hardly breathe fire.

Oh, who could forget the Tucker Torpedo.

In the 50's, you could tell cars apart by the size and pitch of their tail fins. The 1959 Cadillac looked like heron taking flight. And what now? Ugly little wings called spoilers. Just what do they do, prevent the car from flying away? Not much, unless they are massive ones on racing cars. Spoiler is an appropriate description, I think.

Except for a few subtle differences (some have more bulbous noses), a Jaguar is now a Buick, is now BMW, is now a Toyota and, ya sure, even a Volvo.

The new car season in the autumn once rivaled the new seasons of television and football. Van Ness Avenue in San Francisco was once a grand auto row reminiscent of a Paris boulevard. The new model years were debuted with searchlights, not Gumby-like cylinders flailing at the skies. My neighbor Tom, who is 96, fondly remembers those days when he was a Mercedes dealer on the old Van Ness. He has a 1930 Model A Ford, polished to perfection, in his garage. Sometimes, when I pay him a visit, we both stand and quietly admire it.

"Want to buy it?" Tom asked me last week.

Time To Board: Stoner Airline Flight 420

Welcome aboard Stoner Airlines Flight 420 to mile-high Denver with ongoing service to Weed, California and Maui-Wowie.

I'm your pilot Buzz *One Giant Step Into Thin Air* Doobie. Your flight attendant is Mary Jane.

As this airline has designed this plane to cram as many of you in here as possible, we will do everything possible to ease the pain, especially you who are stacked horizontally in economy. Due to FAA regulations, this is a non-smoking flight, but various treats will be available from the *Dude with the Food* once we get underway.

Today we are offering two channels of entertainment, the classic "Up in Smoke" starring Cheech and Chong on channel one and a National Geographic special on meercats on channel two.

For those of you who would simply like to sleep with your eyes open, the Pink Floyd channel is available...uh...somewhere. Note the purple jellyfish being projected on the walls and ceiling. They will change color as we reach our cruising altitude.

Our little rocketship will just keep on going up and up and up until we reach 130 thousand feet where we may either level off or try something different. Let Mary Jane know if you have any suggestions. Please stash your dime bags under the seat in front of you, fasten your seat belts and don't wander the aisles, open the doors or try to walk on the wings.

So, the sound of the bong means full throttle...its time to flyyyyyy.

Disregard the rattle, we are climbin' real fast. Gotta light load today, plenty of good gas and no seagulls in the engine. Below, starboard, is the island of Manhattan. Oh dang, no, that's the luggage on the tarmac. Whatever. It'll catch up.

We know you have a choice, we thank you for choosing Stoner Airlines. "We make flying... flying again."

WHEN TIMES WERE SIMPLER
Heavens to Betsy, or is it Mergatroyd?

I have two elderly aunts, Aunt Betsy and Miss Mergatroyd. They live in a double bungalow on Elm street, under two oak trees, with their nine cats and a parrot named Casanova.

Aunt Betsy finished college early with her Mrs. degree.

Miss Mergatroyd was a successful entrepreneur, founding Miss Mergatroyd's School of Typing and Manners.

Now they sit in their parlor amongst their pots of African violets, which rest on lace doilies, and reminisce about the good old days.

"Fred, rest his soul. I miss him so much, our rides on *the old jalopy*," said Betsy.

"Oh yes, said Miss Mergatroyd, "the one with the running board, like Eliot Ness stood on when he was chasing Capone. *It went like sixty.*"

"*Holy Moley*," said Betsy, "you remember that? We were broke all the time, not exactly living *the life of Riley*. And Fred did go out on his benders, but every time he tied one on, *I hung him out to dry* and life became, more or less, *hunky dory*. Yes, we were *in like Flynn.*"

"*Gee willikers*" said Miss Mergatoyd, "you had the *moxie* to pull through that. I wish that I had such luck, but then, you're Irish. All of my affairs were with *knuckleheads and nincompoops.*"

"And, *jumpin' Jehosaphat*, what about that, Bobby? *Such a pill*", said Betsy.

"Bobby was *the straw that broke the camel's back*," said Miss Mergatroid, "After Bobby, I *woke up and smelled the roses*. Oh I did have one brief fling with Kilroy, but he was never here. After that, to quote the raven, never more, *not for all the tea in China.*"

"But, Heavens to Mergatroyd," said Betsy, "we still have each other.

"*Heavens to Betsy*," said Mergatroyd, "so we do."

Connected Traveler Magazine

connectedtraveler.com

GONE ASTRAY PODCAST
on all major podcast networks

Photos,Video
russelljohnson.com

Russ Johnson and Pat Meier-Johnson being scrutinized by their editor.

Russell Johnson began his career in high school as a disc jockey, moving on to CBS's WCCO-TV in Minneapolis where he did satirical bits on a show called The Bedtime Nooz, celebrated as being a forerunner of Saturday Night Live, followed by a career as a broadcast journalist in Sacramento and San Francisco and more than thirty years as an independent film and video producer for clients ranging from American Express and luxury cruise lines to the United Nations and the Asian Development Bank. His work took him to some 60 countries.

Over the years, he has contributed features to public radio in the US and is Editor and Publisher of The Connected Traveler, one of the premiere web magazines, which Lonely Planet called "Armchair travel at its best." He is host of the humor podcast Gone Astray, and author of the book and audio book "Tales of the Radio Traveler."

Made in the USA
Monee, IL
24 December 2024

72103668R00046